The 99 Names of Allah

SENAD TOPCAGIC

To order additional copies of this book, contact:
Xlibris
1-800-455-039
www.xlibris.com.au
Orders@Xlibris.com.au

ISBN: 978-1-9845-0575-0 (sc)
ISBN: 978-1-9845-0576-7 (e)

Print information available on the last page

Rev. date: 03/25/2020

The
99 Names
of Allah

Ar-Rahman

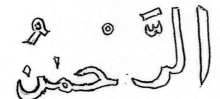

The Most Gracious

Allah

One God

Al-Malik

The True King

Ar-Rahim

The Most Merciful

Ar-Salam

The Source of Peace

Al-Qudoos

The Most Holy

Al-Muhaiman

The Protector

Al-Mu'min

The Most Faithful

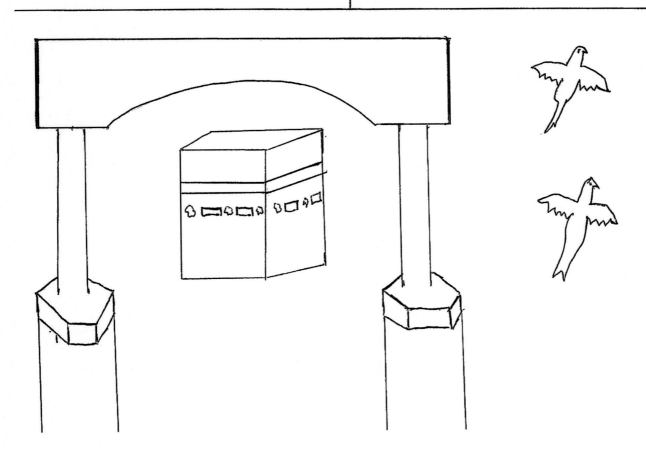

Al-Jabbar

الْجَبَّار

The Compeller

Al-'Azeez

الْعَزِيز

The ever-Mighty

Al-Khaaliq

الْخَالِق

The Creator

Al-Mutakabbir

الْمُتَكَبِّر

The Majestic

Al-Mussawwir

The Fashioner

Al-Baari

The Originator

Al-Qahhar

The Subduer

Al-Ghaffaar

The Forgiver

Al-Razzaaq

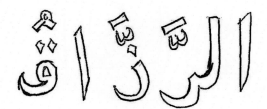

The Provider

Al-Wahhab

The Bestower

Al-'Aleem

The All Knowing

Al-Fattah

The Opener

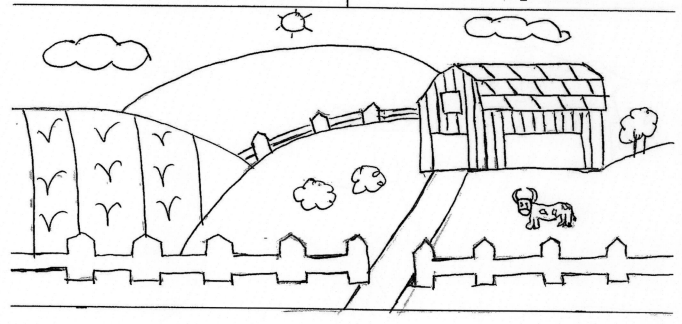

Al-Baasit

الْبَاسِطُ

The Expander

Al-Qaabid

الْقَابِضُ

The Withholder

Ar-Raafi'

الرَّافِعُ

The Exalter

Al-Khaafidh

الْخَافِضُ

The Abaser

Al-Muzil
الْمُزِلْ
The Humiliator

Al-Mu'izz
الْمُعِزْ
The Bestower

Al-Baseer
الْبَصِيْرْ
The All Seeing

As-Samee'
السَّمِيْعْ
The All Hearing

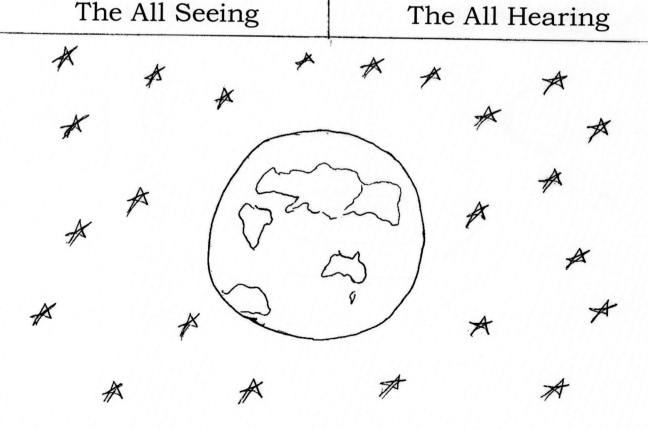

Al-'Adl

The Just

Al-Hakam

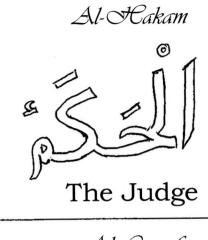

The Judge

Al-Khabeer

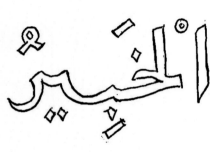

The All Aware

Al-Lateef

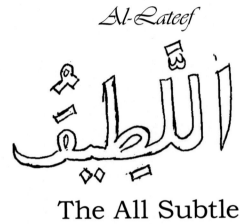

The All Subtle

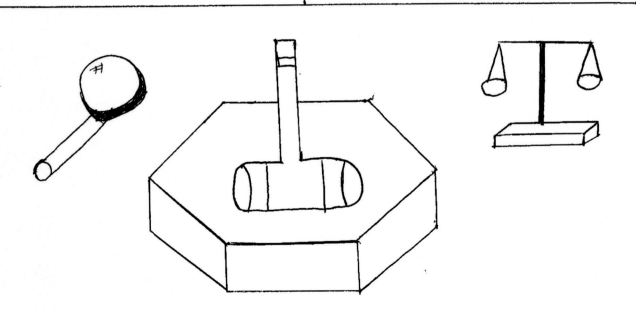

Al-'Atheem

The Supreme

Al-Haleem

The Forbearing

Ash-Shakoor

The Appreciative

Al-Ghafoor

The Forgiving

Al Quran

Al-Kabeer

الْكَبِيْر

The Most Great

Al-'Alee

الْعَلِيّ

The Most High

Al-Mugeet

الْمُقِيْت

The Sustainer

Al-Hafeedh

الْحَفِيْظ

The Preserver

Al-Jaleel

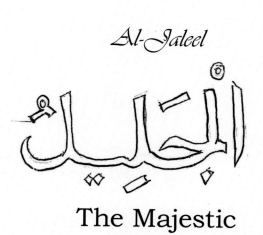

The Majestic

Al-Haseeb

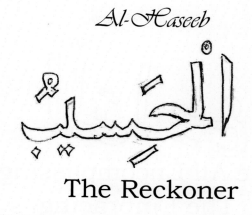

The Reckoner

Ar-Raqeeb

The Watchful

Al-Kareem

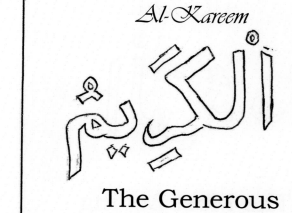

The Generous

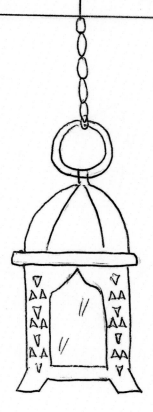

Al-Waasi'

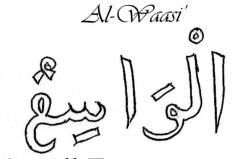

The All Encompassing, The Embracing

Al-Mujeeb

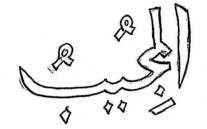

The Responsive

Al-Wadood

The Most Loving

Al-Hakeem

The Wise

Al-Ba'ith

الْبَاعِث

The Resurrector

Al-Majeed

الْمَجِيد

The Glorious

Al-Haqq

الْحَقّ

The Truth

Ash-Shaheed

الشَّهِيد

The Witness

ARAFAT

Al-Qawiyy

The Most Strong

Al-Wakeel

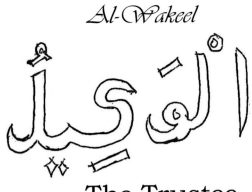

The Trustee

Al-Waliyy

The Protector

Al-Mateen

The Firm One

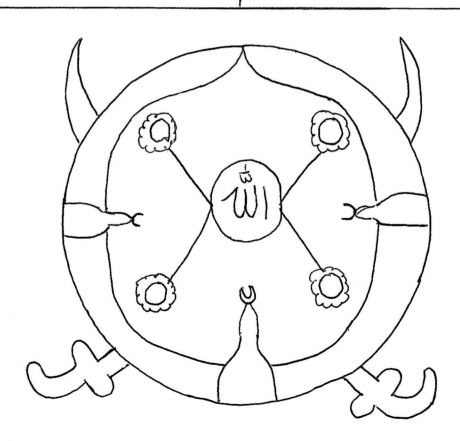

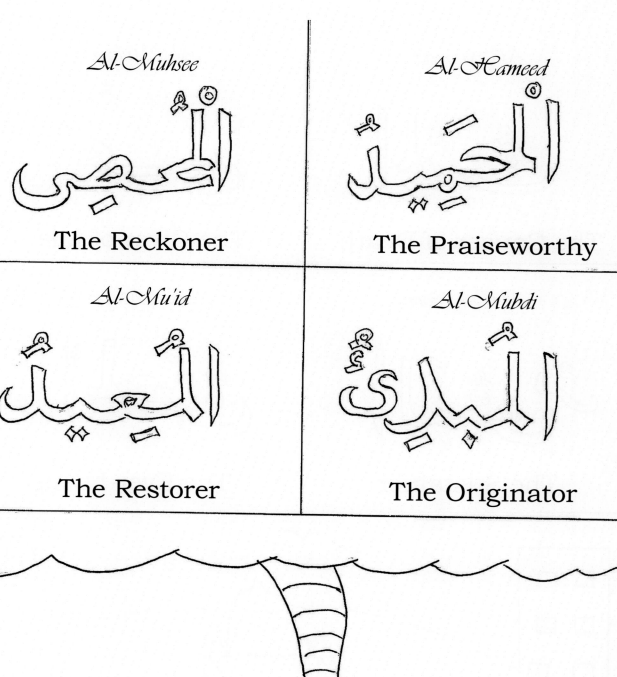

Al-Muhsee

The Reckoner

Al-Hameed

The Praiseworthy

Al-Mu'id

The Restorer

Al-Mubdi

The Originator

Al-Mumeet

The Causer of Death

Al-Muhyee

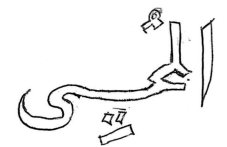

The Giver of Life

Al-Qayyoom

The Sustainer

Al-Hayy

The Ever-Living

Al-Maajid

The Noble

Al-Wajid

The Perceiver

Al-Ahad

The One

Al-Waahid

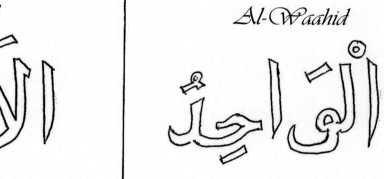

The Unique

Al-Qadeer

الْقَادِرُ

The Capable

As-Samad

الصَّمَدُ

The Eternal

Al-Muqaddim

الْمُقَدِّمُ

The Expediter

Al-Muqtadir

الْمُقْتَدِرُ

The Powerful

Al-Awwal

الْأَوَّلُ

The First

Al-Mu'akhkhir

The Delayer

Az-Dhaahir

The Manifest

Al-Aakhir

The Last

Al-Waali

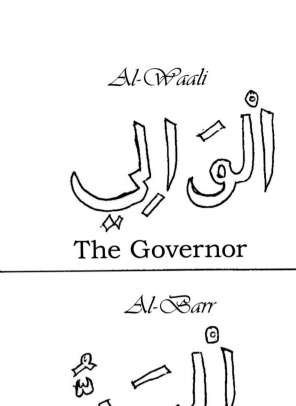

The Governor

Al-Baatin

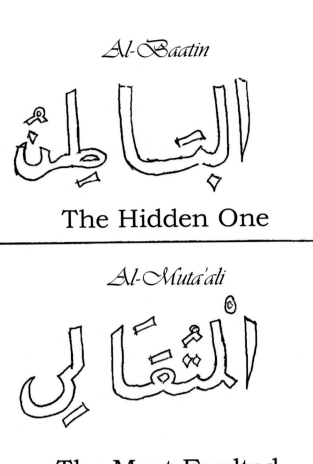

The Hidden One

Al-Barr

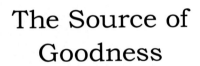

The Source of
Goodness

Al-Muta'ali

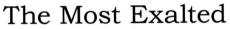

The Most Exalted

Al-Muntaqim

The Avenger

At-Tawwab

The Ever-Pardoning

Ar-Ra'oof

The Most Kind

Al-'Afuww

The Pardoner

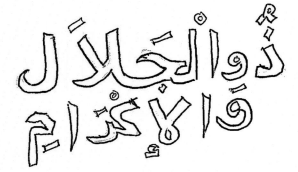

Dhul-Jalaali Wal-Ikraam

Possessor of Majesty
and Honour

Maalik-ul-Mulk

Owner
of the
Kingdom

Al-Jaami'

The Gatheror

Al-Muqsit

The Just

Al-Mughni

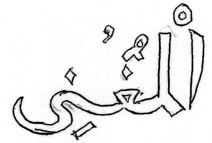

The Enricher

Al-Ghaniyy

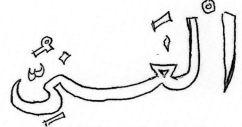

The Self Sufficient

Ad-Dhaar

The Distresser

Al-Mani'

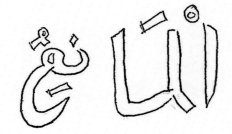

The Withholder

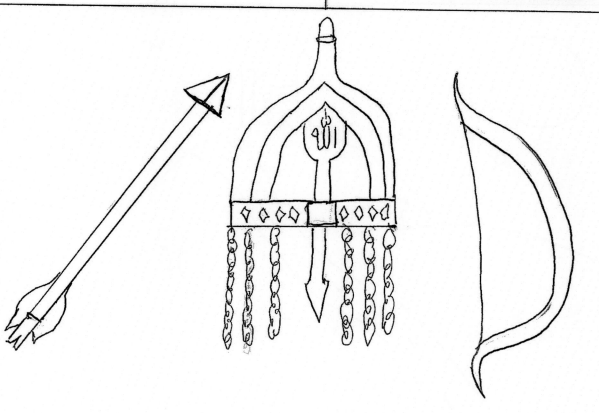

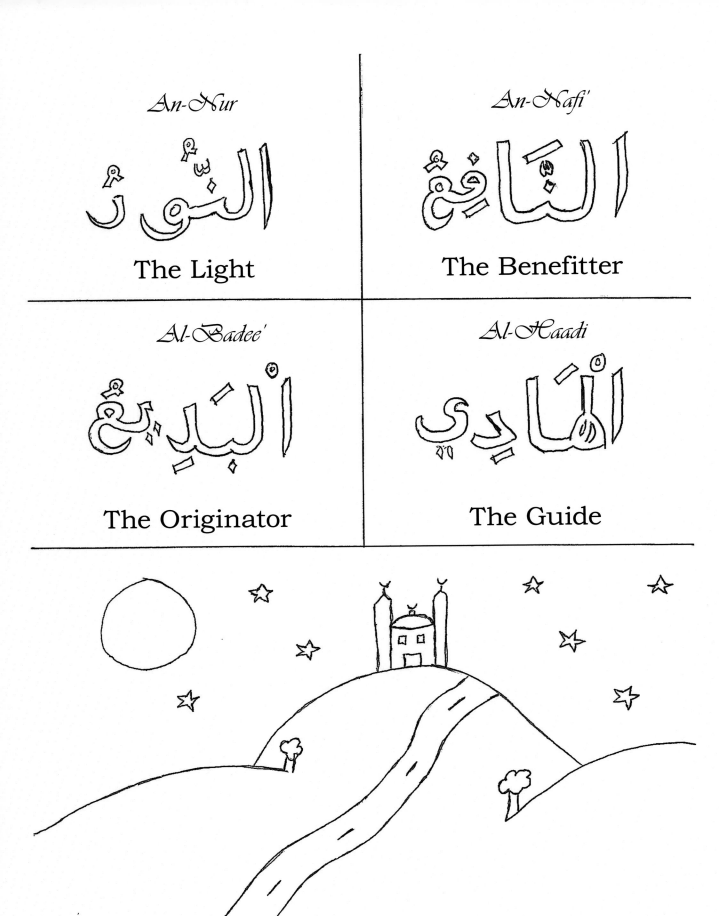

An-Nur

النُّورُ

The Light

An-Nafi'

النَّافِعُ

The Benefitter

Al-Badee'

الْبَدِيعُ

The Originator

Al-Haadi

الْهَادِى

The Guide

Al-Waarith
ٱلْوَارِثُ

The Inheritor

Al-Baaqi
ٱلْبَاقِي

The Ever Lasting

As-Saboor
ٱلصَّبُورُ

The Patient

Ar-Rasheed
ٱلرَّشِيدُ

The Guide

Printed in the United States
By Bookmasters